Painfully Sane

By Emily H. Sturgill

2019

Poetry and Artwork

Painfully Sane-

I. Poetry and Art

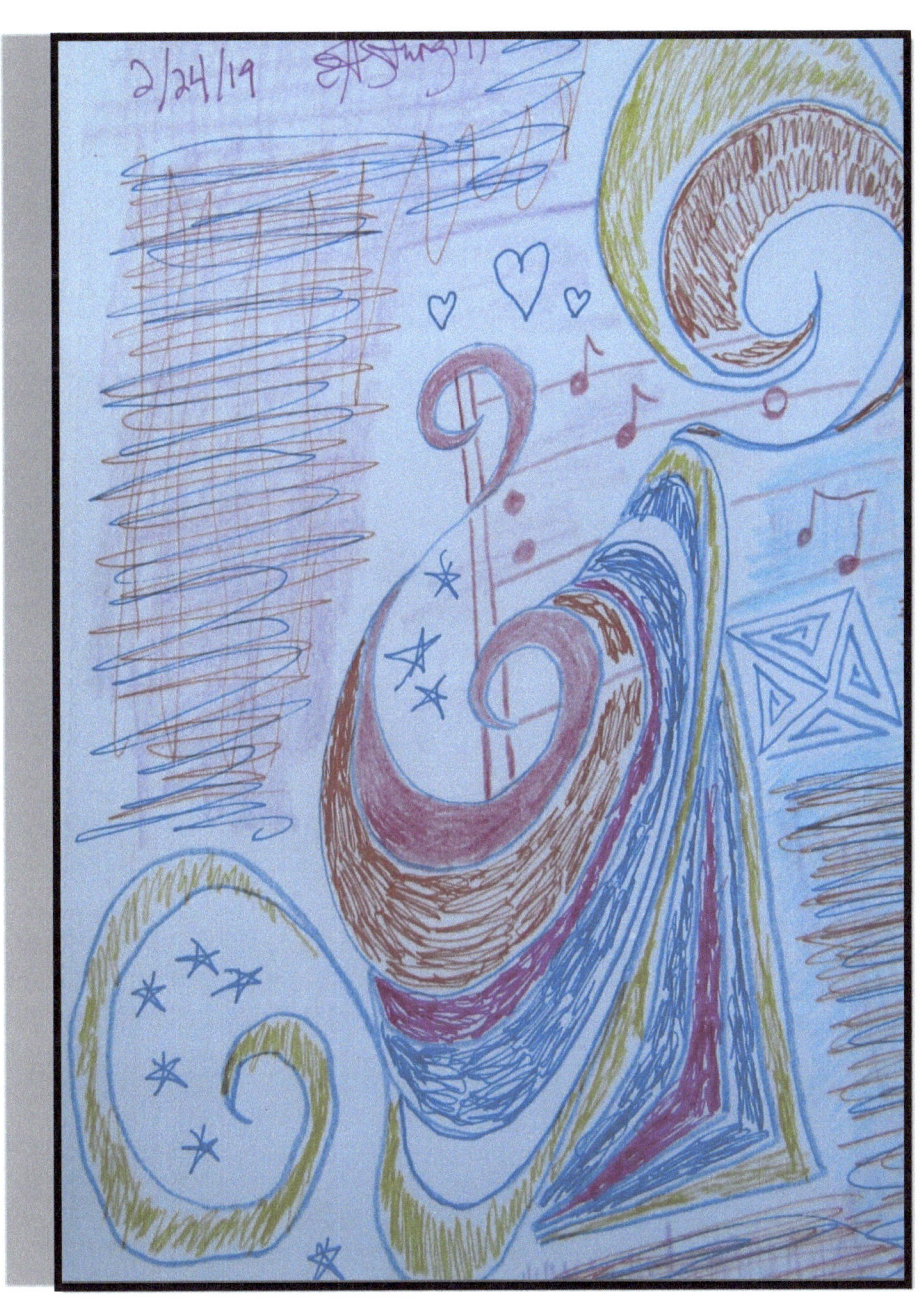

Making Magic- 10/21/18

Published on www.sexinthekitchensink.wordpress.com

Words fall out

rapidly like a fire hose.

Words fall down,

Sideways, stumble, stretching

into a staircase.

Words bubble upwards,

lifting my soul

higher and higher.

Words flake off,

lightly longingly into

a stream of

subconscious poetry.

A Nonsense Song- 6/8/19

Morning coffee

black as sin

hot as summer

where words begin.

Just out of grasp

desperate

to pluck

petals of poetry.

Falling so loose

And flying

into the wind.

Ideas and Metaphors

beginning to Spin,

into a flight of fanasty.

Fistfuls of flowers

Strange strangulation

Of words-without the warmth

Of sunlight.

Poetry seems empty

As I drink my morning coffee.

Morning coffee

Black as sin

Hot as summer

where words begin.

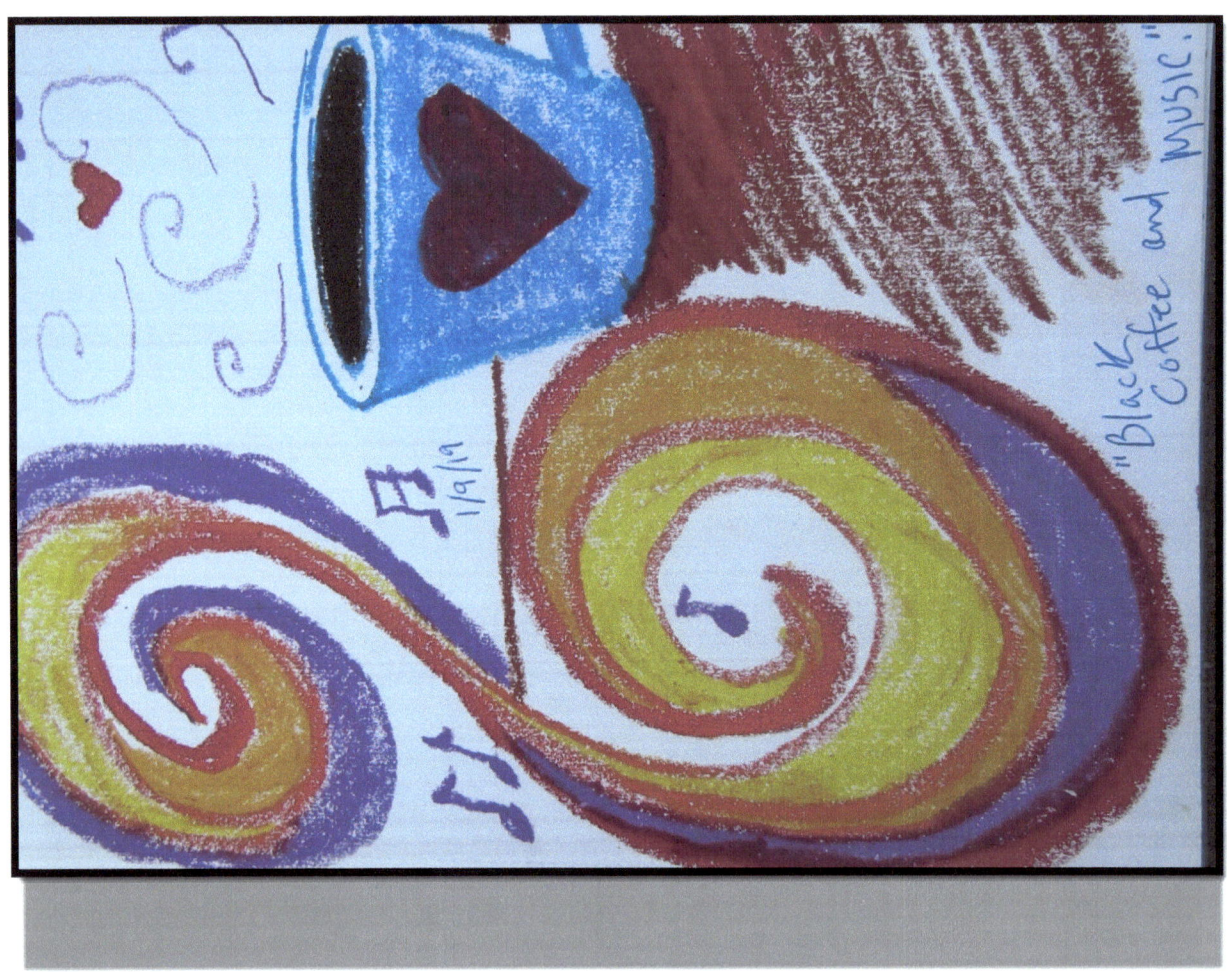

Medusa   4/2/19

Mythological

Eruptions of

Damnation.

Universal unity

Serpentine spikes solid sharpen statues

Angelic in chaos wake.

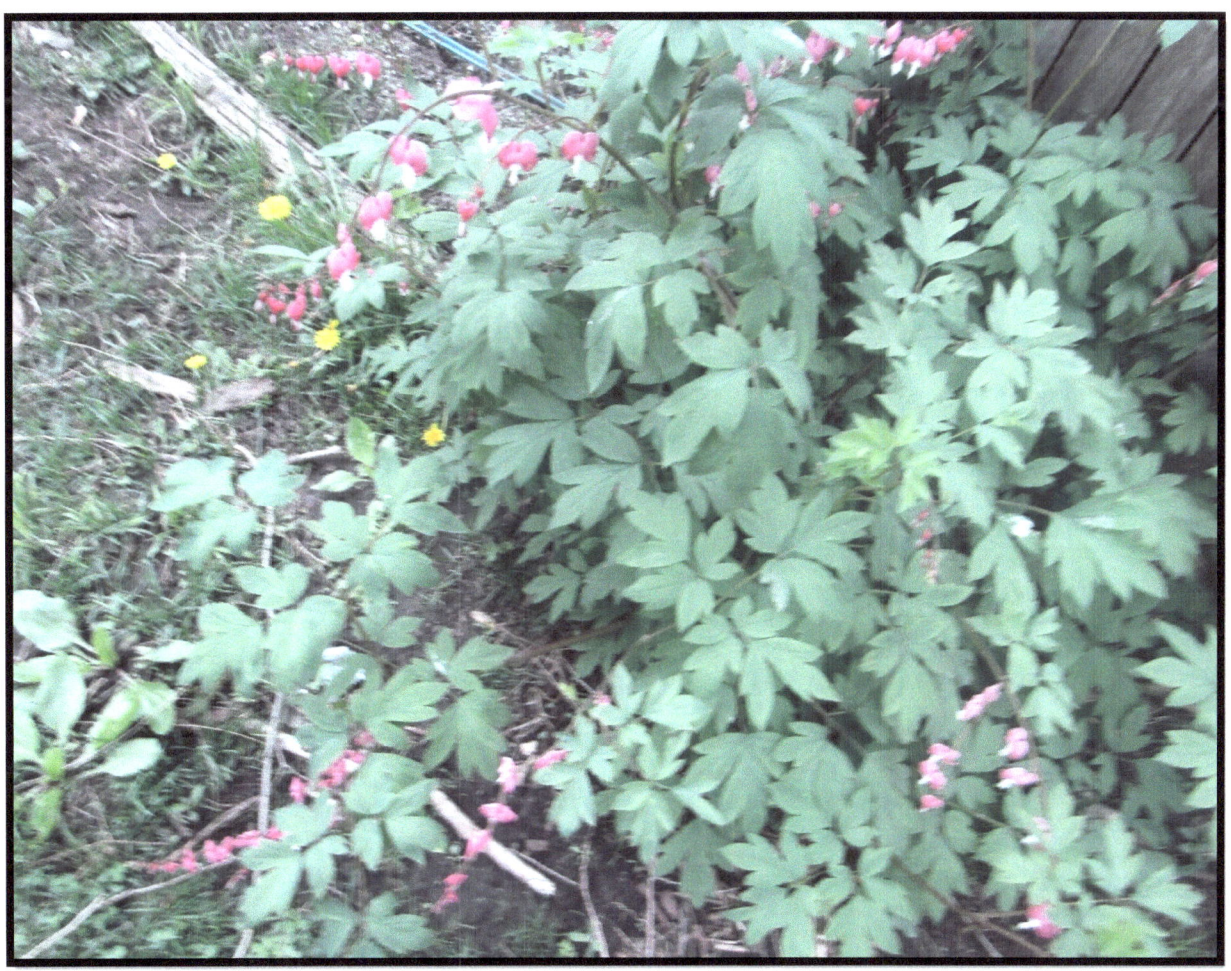

Imagination- 2/27/19

Imagination

Illustrations

Dancing beyond

the curtain

is a blank white page.

 Poetry unspoken

artworks neglected as the clock,

gallops past.

Time is a fine fast horse.

Time is sometimes a thief,

as we forget

it's limitations.

Imagination

Illustrations,

dancing beyond the curtain.

Creation is a Shadow,

a collection of Ego.

I am waiting for my Shadow

To speak,

Words like petals,

blowing loose in the wind.

Lips- 3/3/19

The taste of

butterscotch.

The flavor of words,

dripping from fresh

redden lips,

teeth gnashing on vowels

as music.

Mouthing metaphors,

The sky is a simile.

The snow of March

Hard like an apple

Crunchy like broken Earth.

Ideas perish like petals.

Withering in ice

Words dripping from

Fresh redden lips and

Teeth gnashing on vowels

As music mouthing metaphors

The sky is a simile.

But poetry waits for Spring.

Dirty Hands- March 1st 2019

published on www.sexinthekitchensink.wordpress.com

Spirals of songs

ringing into my mp3 ears

songstruck grabbing at bits and pieces

lyrics licking the palms

of dirty hands.

the gift of singular melody

ringing into my mp3 ears

grabbing at puzzles reaching for words

hearing everything like the first time

lyrics licking the palms

of dirty hands.

sooner than later

dancing will lead to poetry

then it will lead to twisting

and bending into art supplies

lingering music towards motion

sketchbooks opening without pause

these lyrics licking the palms

will lead to drawing

oil pastels or pencils or charcoal

covering these dirty hands.

Words become- 4/12/19

Words cascade

Falling like liquid

Pouring from

The driest lips.

Words are water.

Clear ,clean, clarity.

Flowing like a faucet

You've turned it on

And words tumble.

Words like beads,

strung around my neck

without clear meaning

they are like pearls.

Mythology is a Metaphor.

Words are an accessory.

Description is Language.

And Words are of Sand.

Fine grains clumped together

On a blank page-muddy messy forming

An allegory of verse and rhyme

Words become poetry.

II. Endometriosis

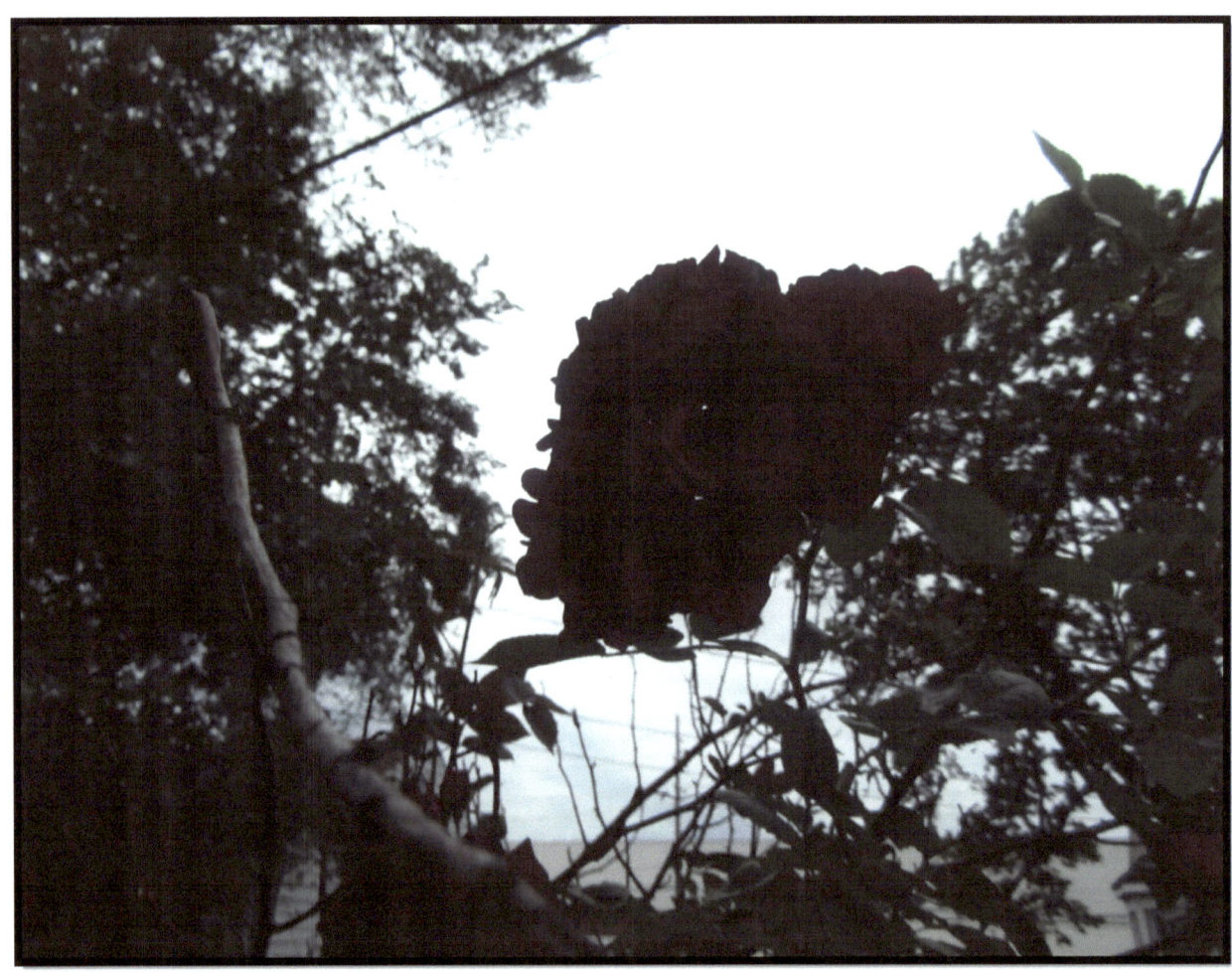

2/8/19   published on www.sexinthekitchensink.wordpress.com

Surreal stabbing pain-

Surreal stabbing pain

my Uterus is bothering me again.

Endometriosis rears it's ugly head.

I feel a cramping sharpened stabbing feeling

in my abdomen back and thighs.

and the monthly agony of bleeding is back,

There are no words for this type of pain except for

overwhelming.....surreal stabbing pain

my uterus is bothering me again.

Puddles of Pain...4/2/19

Published on www.sexinthekitchensink.wordpress.com

twisted torso of torsion.

ugly uterus untrustworthy.

a sea of infertility.

blood bleeding brightly

into

puddles of pain.

my fifth day still twisting

turning into knots this-

ugly uterus untrustworthy

due to endometriosis.

heating pads, electric blanket and Tylenol

mere essentials for survival as my body rebels

attacking me monthly.

6/19/19

Pain paves my way-

Published on www.sexinthekitchensink.wordpress.com

Pain paves my way

It passes over my body

In bent and twisted ways.

It follows me everywhere.

For at least 1/4 of every month.

I try to fight it.

Heated blankets and Tylenol.

I usually lose the fight.

Pain knows all the tricks.

Pain fights dirty breaks the rules.

Pain is part of my journey and

It whispers secrets just to me.

Pain paves my way.

The Empty-2/27/19

An empty shell,

An half-cracked egg,

Split blood and a full moon.

An unspoken spell.

Many years left untouched,

Between the seams

Of two miscarriages and

A sea of infertility.

There lies an empty

Woman

Longing to grow

A seed.

Among barren earth

All that remains

Is a dream

And so much earth.

Broken Flower- 3/29/19

Broken flower

But only so an hour.

The rushing rustle of red petals-

Dropping like blood.

Cracked and curved- a cycle of 28 days.

Moaning in pain, this red rain

Won't delay.

Shaking my uterus to its center to its depths,

As walls of secret and darkness

Collapse into a

Broken flower but only so an hour.

Broken- by Emily H. Sturgill 1/10/19

published on www.sexinthekitchensink.wordpress.com

Broken Brain

Bipolar disorder broke my brain in two poles.

With my medications I walk a tightrope between these poles

depression and mania.....I try daily to slip into the in-between-ness of these two things.

medicine helps but it does not cure. It only helps to contain a balance of semi-stability.

So yes I've got a broken brain.

Also I've got a broken Uterus. I have Endometriosis Stage 4. A fancy way of brokenness...

I hurt a lot of the time. It's the worst whenever I am bleeding. Crumpled into layers of pain cramping aching stabbing screaming agony of pain. I'm hurting today in fact. Despite my period not due for two more days my broken uterus spits brownish blood and I know that means to hell with the calendars my period's starting early. Up until 2015 I was taking codeine for the pain. Then I went through the process of applying for a medical marijuana card. I got off codeine. Now instead of pain daily from my endometriosis I've only got pain during my periods and during ovulation.....

A broken Uterus. A history of Infertility. Two pregnancies=Two miscarriages.

It's a fancy form of broke-ness. It's a double whammy. A broken brain. A broken Uterus.

But deep down inside beneath all of the broken things is my poetry is my stories is my spirit and my soul-even beneath all of that is my heart which is strong unflinching warm and consistently unbroken. It beats on and on-unbroken. And beneath this broken brain and broken uterus is an unbroken girl grasping at straws and pulling like weeds from the ground fist-fills of words which fall to my feet into puddles of poetry.

II.   Manic Depression

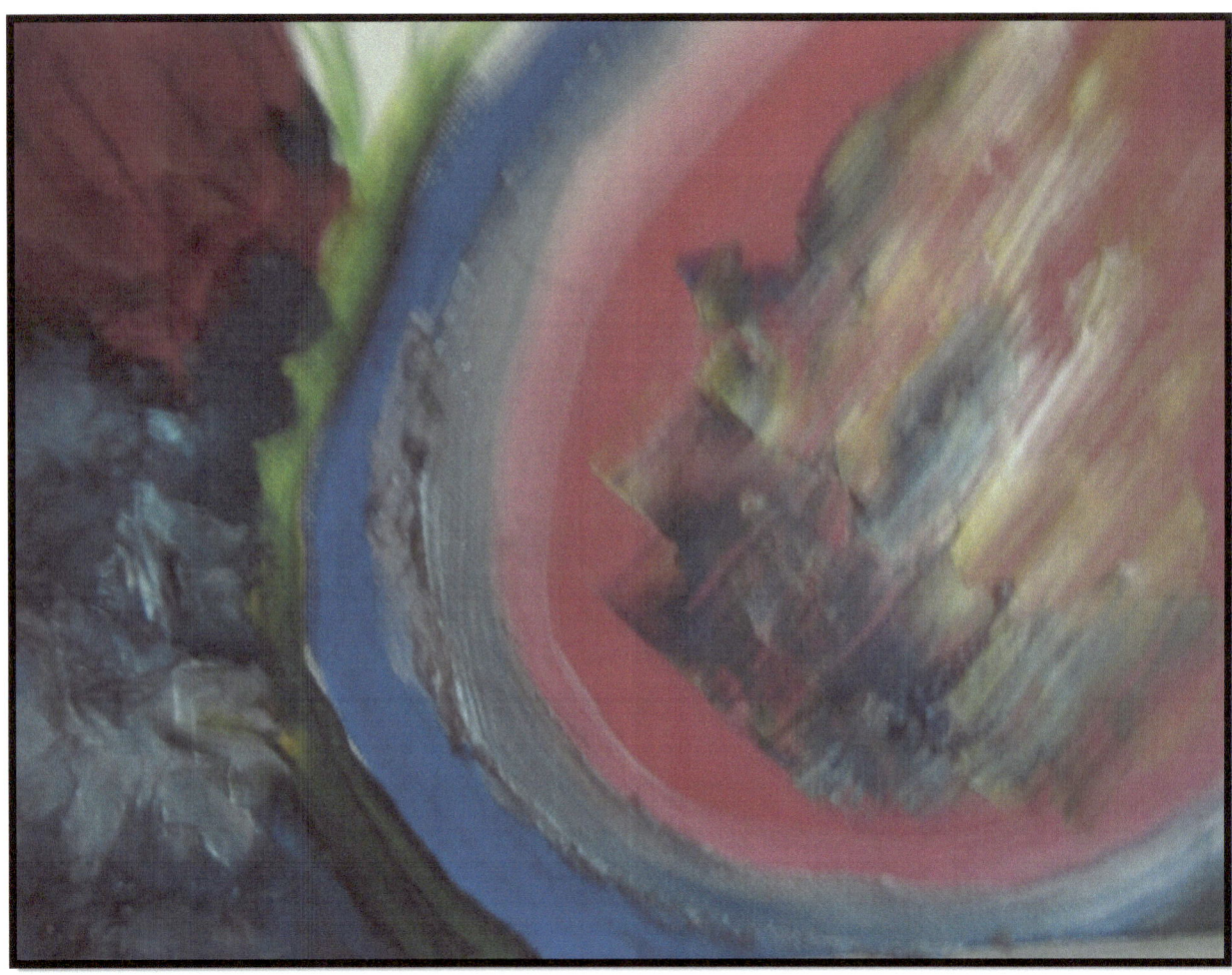

III.

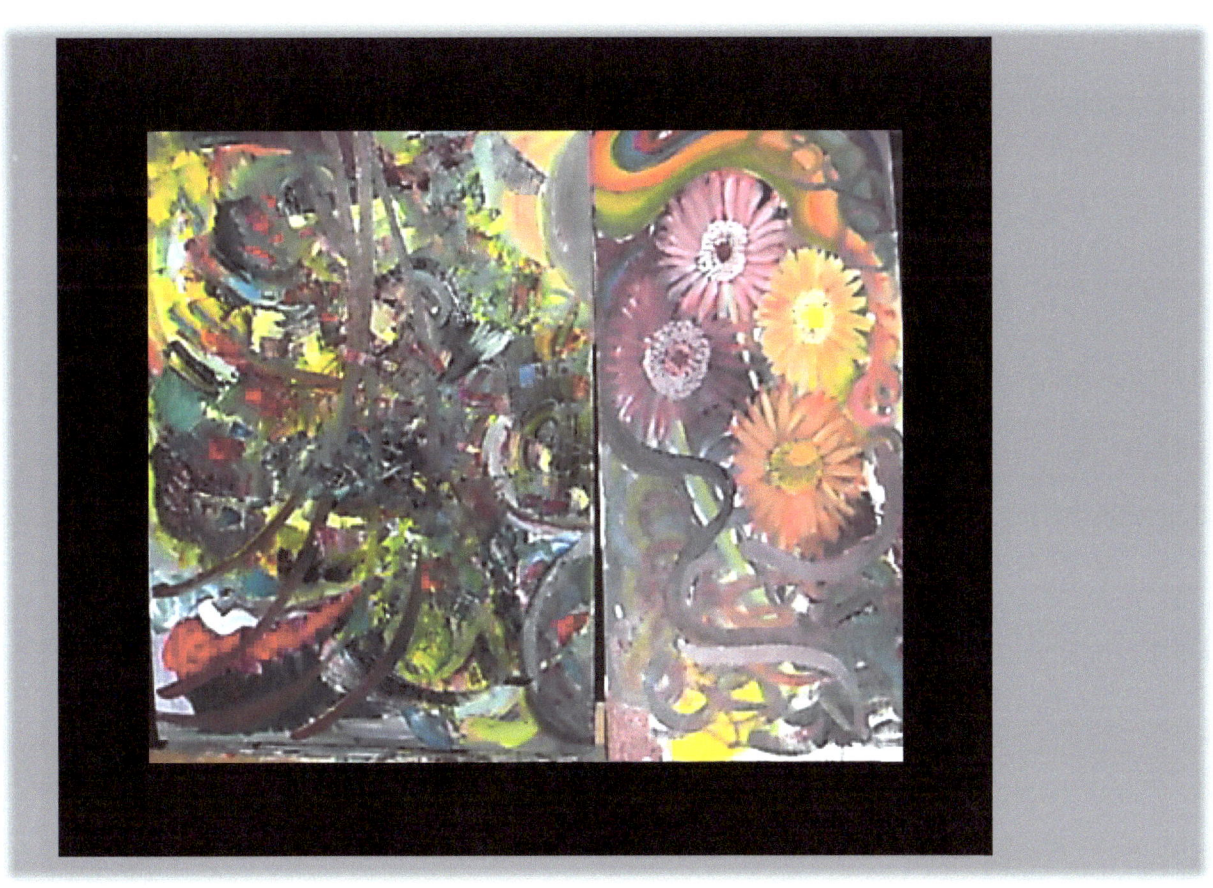

Swimming with Sharks 6/15/19

Published on www.sexinthekitchensink.wordpress.com

Summer brings warmer waters.

Summer welcomes beautiful oceans,

and breathless seas.

Sandy white beaches, scattered sea shells and

thrilling deep diving.

Summer brings tranquility, solace and happiness.

Be wary of that deep dive and all those thrills however...

Summer's warm waters also brings

sharks closer to the shores.

Before you know it if you're not careful

you'll be swimming with sharks

turning the beauty of the ocean

into a scarlet tide

not only dark red deep

but terrifying

what once was so beautiful

can turn on you

you'll be lucky if you make it out alive.

you'll be lucky if you survive.

and that's how I feel

as I struggle with my manic-depression.

It contains all the beauty of the entire ocean

but the sharks swim there too.

Balance   6/15/19

Published on www.sexinthekitchensink.wordpress.com

There is a tightrope I walk

it covers miles of canyons

which sink to depths I've never seen.

And the sky above is vast and huge

those tall summit heights I'll never climb.

But the in-between is my tightrope.

I'm very fortunate to have a safety net

consisting of family, friends and even some strangers

off the internet.

This is all in place

just in case I stumble or fall.

It's my saving grace.

I've been walking this same tightrope

since I was only 18.

Despite being terrified of heights,

I must continue walking this rope

above great canyons

It's a process, a journey which never ends,

a struggle to find balance.

Climbing 6/8/19

Published on www.sexinthekitchensink.wordpress.com

Haven't showered in days.

Summer sticks to skin, Skin sticks to Skin.

hair is oily

lying in clumps.

motivation is secret and locked under key.

Something so simple

a clean hot shower

getting dressed-

Mt. Everest.

lack of self-care

just a symptom

of my bipolar disorder.

But I can fight.

I can climb those mountains,

(feels like Mt..Everest)

and reach for the rain-

to wash away

all the dirt

of these feelings

to be clean again.

I must grow-   6/8/19

Published on www.sexinthekitchensink.wordpress.com

Bleeding Heart bush

Wildflowers sprouting

Sunlight and green grass.

Dogs playing

a murky pond

yearning for goldfish.

Lily pads and algae.

What does Summer mean to me?

This I do not know

but like everything else

I've planted-

I must grow.

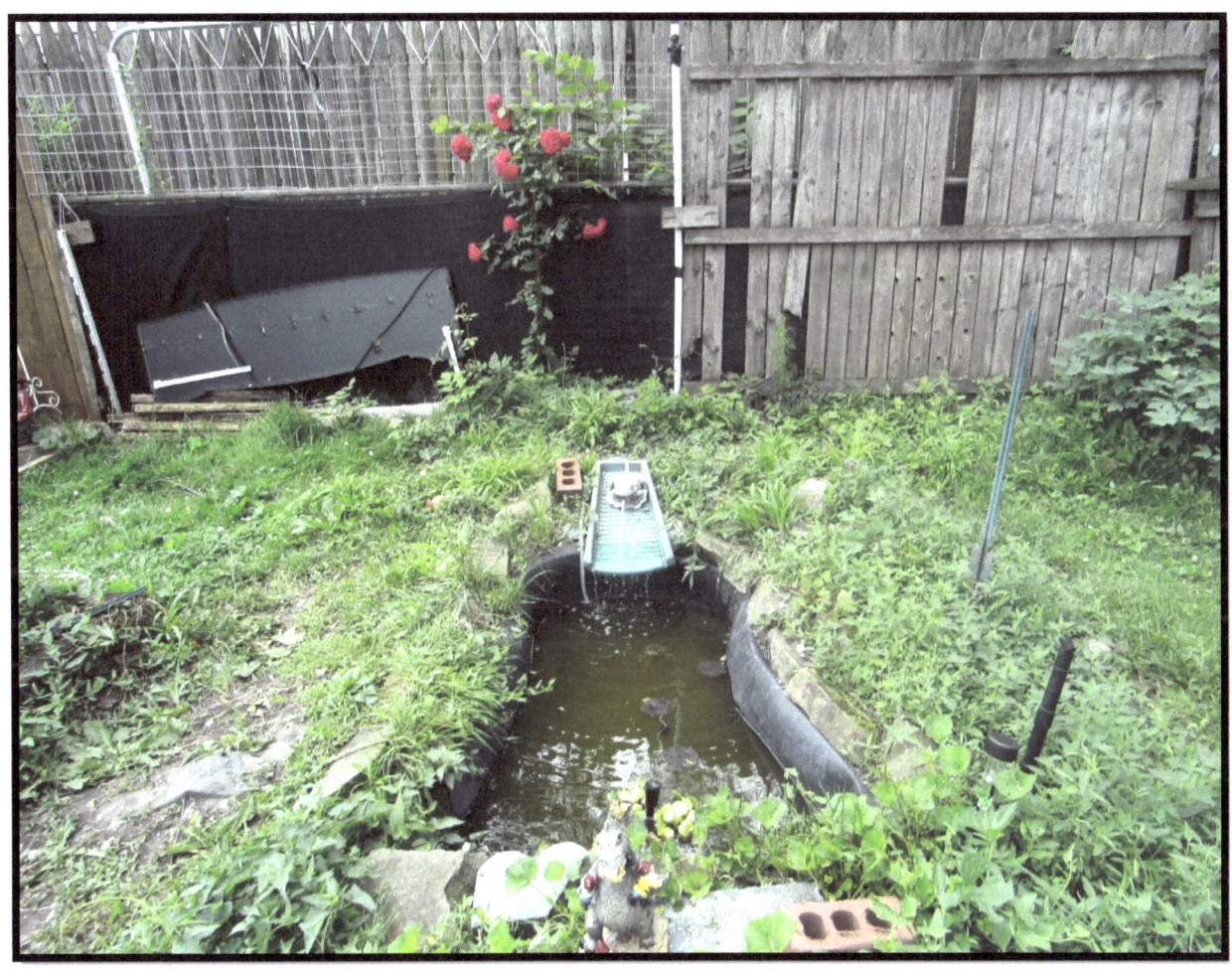

Painfully Sane-5/29/19

I take my bipolar medications,

twice daily.

And I find myself balanced-

a tightrope of Remission of Sorts.

No more wildness. No more delusions of grandeur.

Instead I'm just me and I stick to a routine

I'm no longer depressed I'm no longer manic….but

Those thoughts and memories still chase me.

Instead I am painfully sane. Sanity is indeed painful because

too often I've seen it's opposite and life reminds me that

peaceful times don't last forever and that war inside me?

It will come back someday.

And it is a war,

between up and down.

Right now is the in between time-

the land of the painfully sane.

VI. Nature and Weather

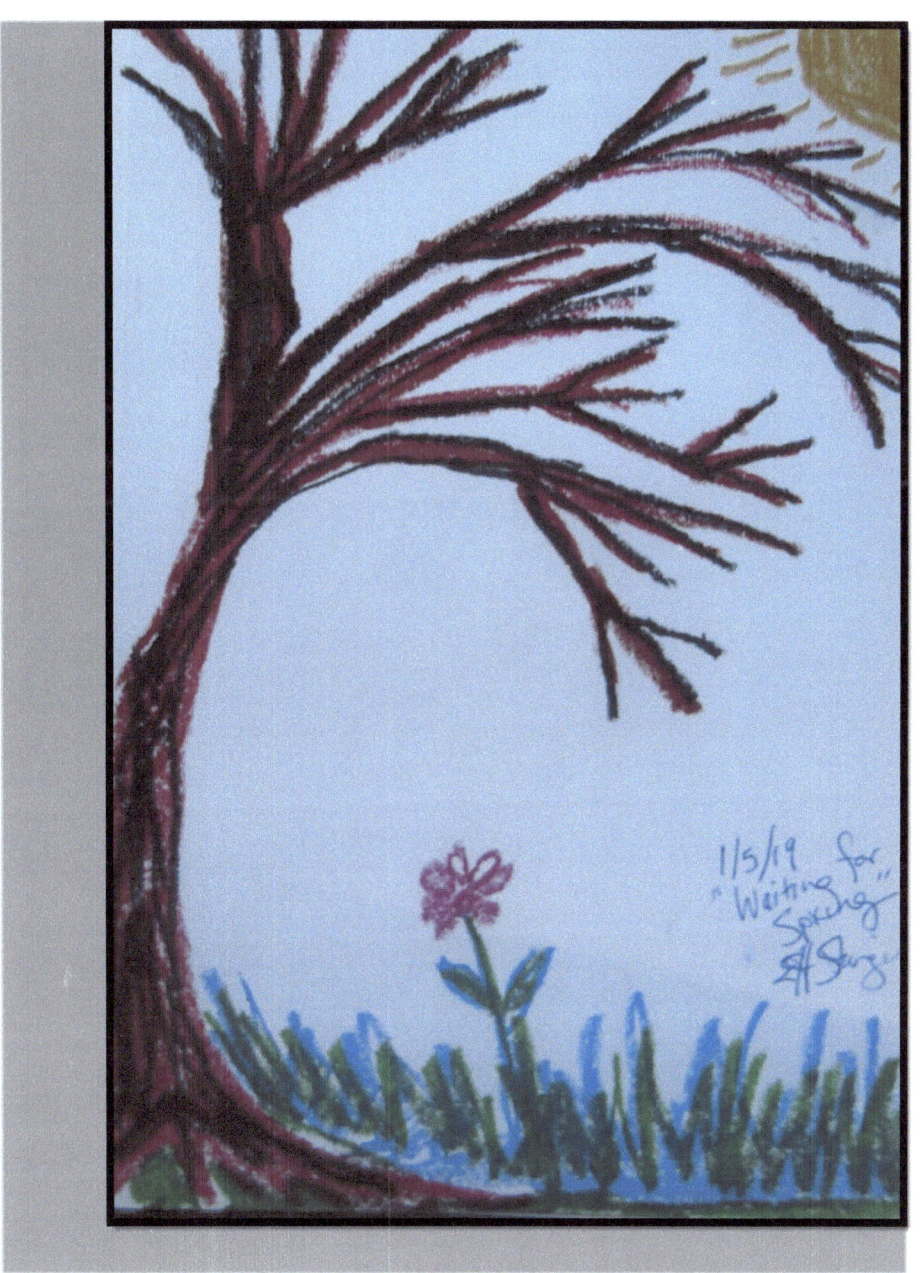

3/1/19   published on www.sexinthekitchensink.wordpress.com

We never know when....

Weds 2/27/19

Michigan Winter

frigid icy solid

snow packed

the firm crunchy carpet

of wet winters bane.

Chilling to the bones

14 degrees brings me

to my knees.

A sea of white harden bone,

spun of velvet.

Snow shatters by a knife of Ice.

Eventually spring will come,

but living in Michigan We never know

when?

Snow sometimes....

March April or May?

The weather just stays this way.

A sea of white harden bone,

spun of velvet.

Snow shatters.....

by a knife of Ice.

Eventually Spring will come.

But living in Michigan,

We never know when?

2-6-19   published on www.sexinthekitchensink.wordpress.com

Winter brings-

Winter brings icy frosted

daydreams of Spring

as I hunger for warmth

I am surrounded by dense frozen cold.

Winter brings harsh cold and blue colored sadness.

I'm living in a Detroit suburb but my heart's in Florida.

where my older sister and my father live....

not my entire heart though simply pieces of it.

The rest of my heart lives here in Michigan with my husband

and our family....but these cold temps, harsh cold and blue colored sadness....

it brings a sort of fleeting depressed madness.

as I hunger for warmth

I am surrounded by dense frozen cold.

Winter brings icy frosted

daydreams of Spring.

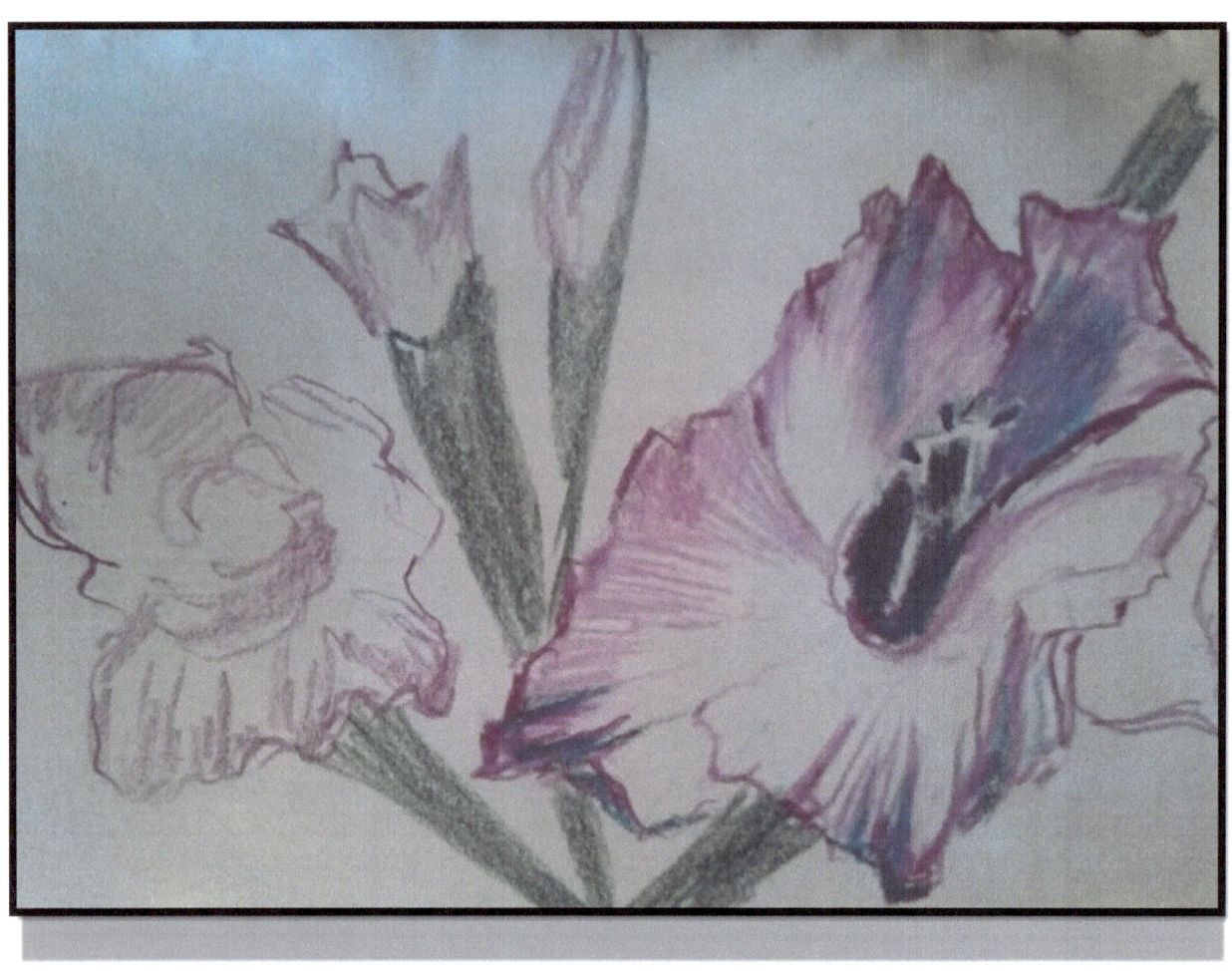

Overlapping Reality- 6/8/19

A collection of white Cobras

Stuck in a Vase.

Barefoot I stumble,

Terrifying tongues touch-

Licking

I open my eyes-wide

As my German Shepherd Isis

Licks my feet.

Surreal

Synchronicity of dreams

Overlapping reality.

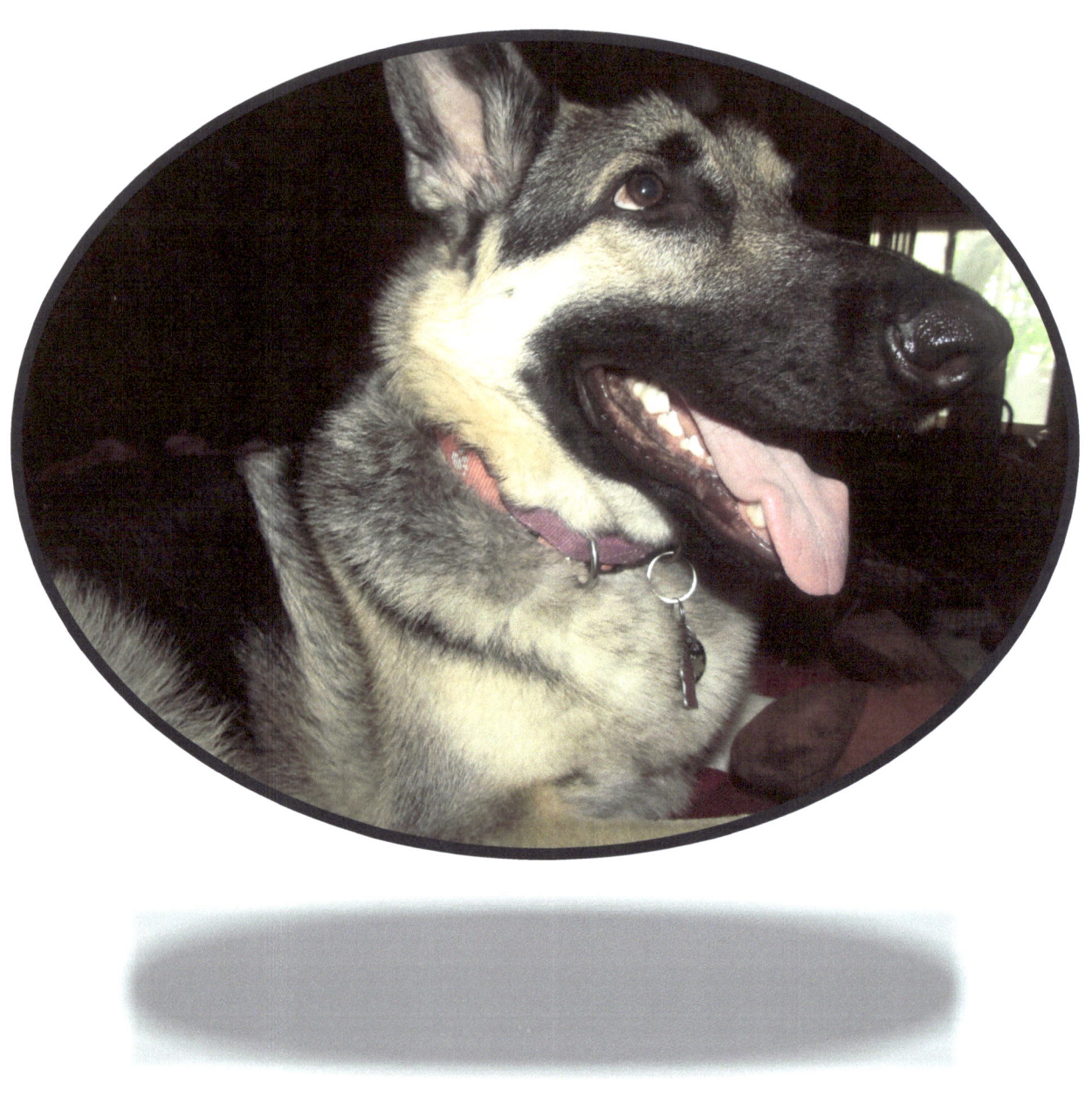

Dearest Isis- 3/29/19

Big triangles

atop a black and tan

head.

Big jagged smile of pearls.

A noble nose interrupted by

The most solemn soulful eyes

Which are the color of honey-brown.

Four large paws,

carrying a broad barrel chest

with a heart too big to contain

all the love within.

Fur flying everywhere.

a sleek long monkey's tail.

She gives me kisses

As I shower her down with

multiple pets.

Beautiful to me.

My loyal friend.

My German Shepherd

Dearest Isis.

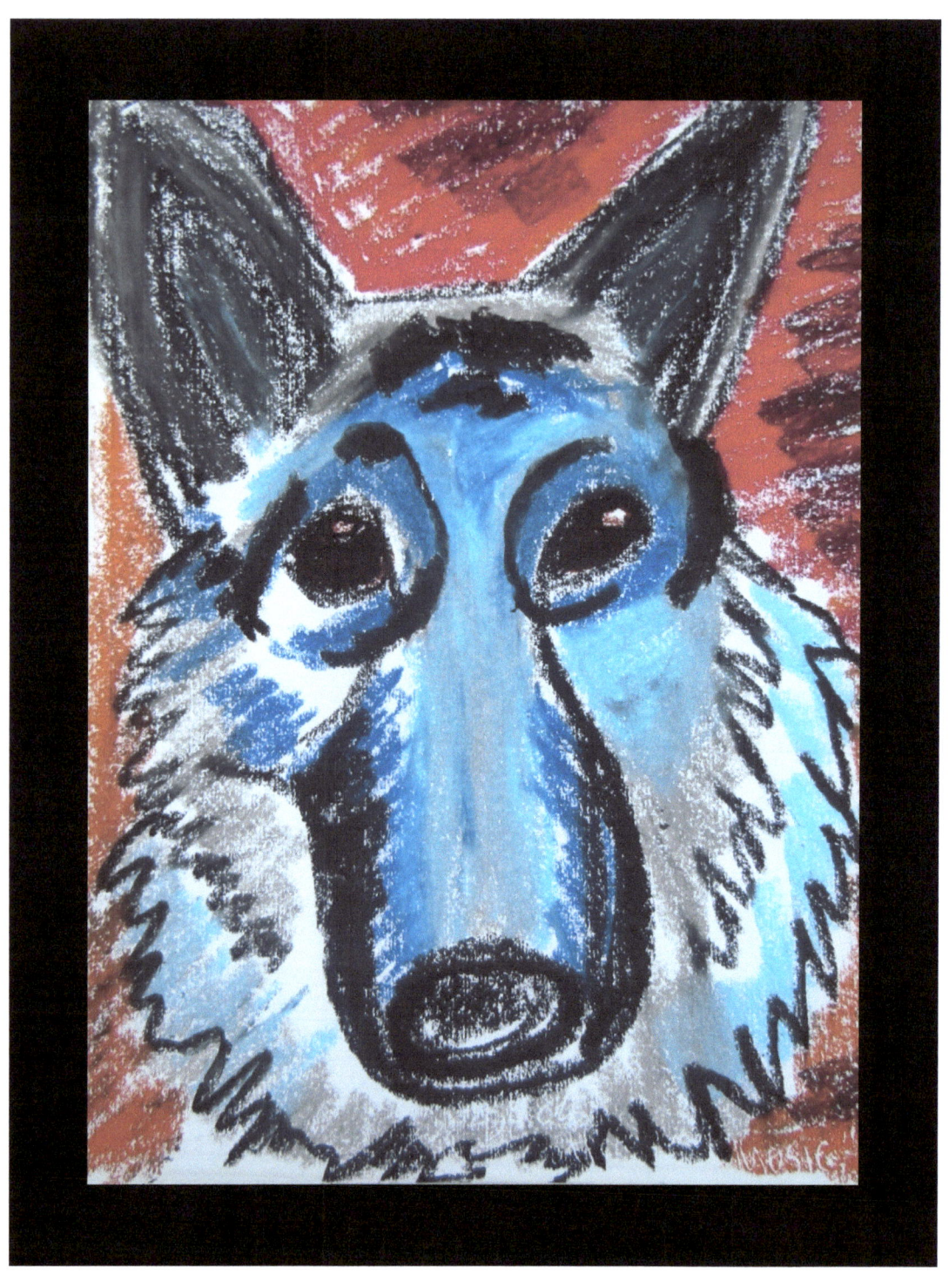

Elemental- 2/27/19

Crystals

Tarot Decks

Amulets

And Incense.

Candles

A circle of salt

A wish

A dream

A blessing and much

uncertainty.

Drinking black coffee

listening to MP3s.

longing for a Mystic.

Longing to be grounded-to walk barefoot,

in the grass and flowers under the Moonlight.

To find my happy place again.

Where the whole world contains Magick

And you only have to close your eyes

To believe it.

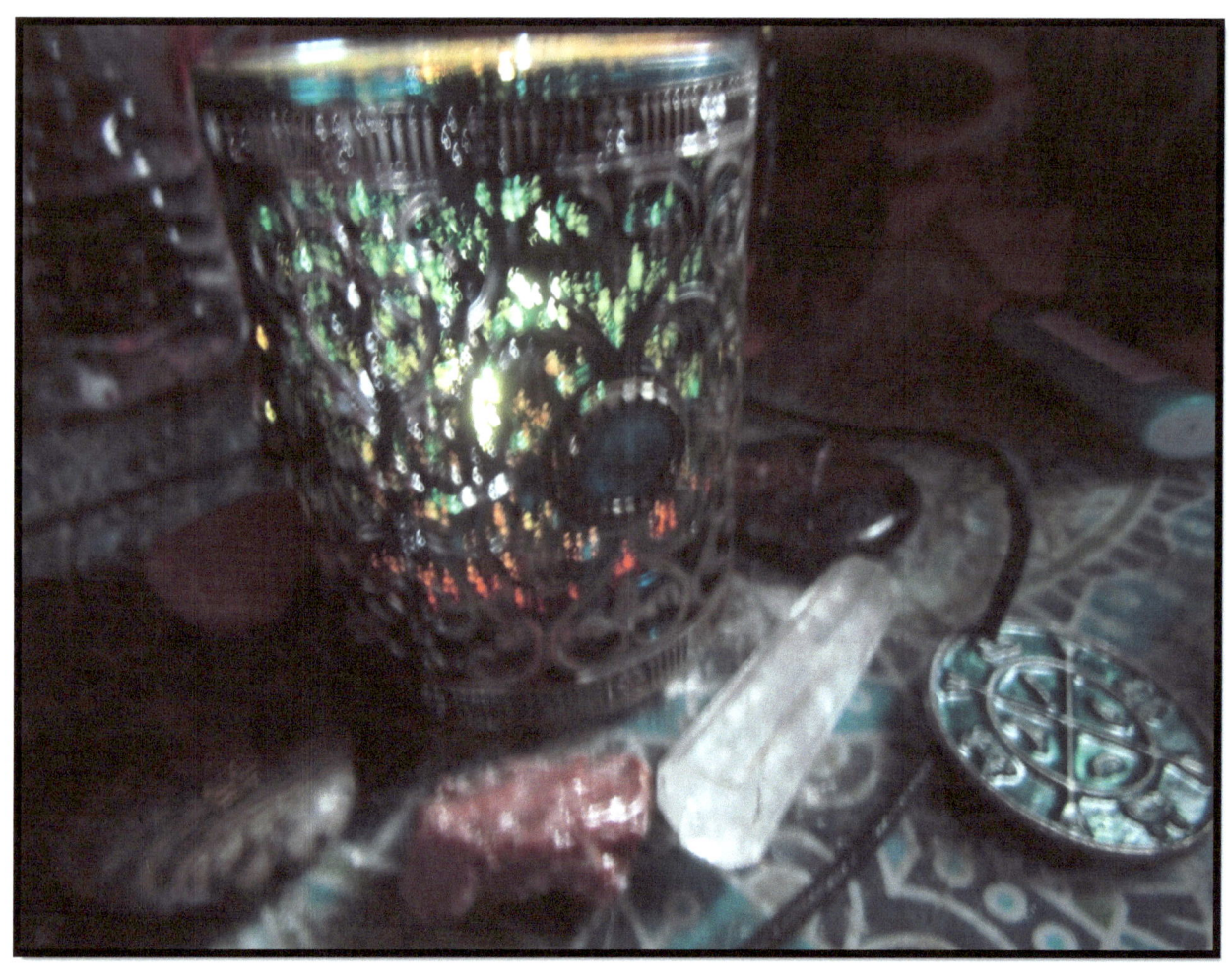

Spellbound 6/8/19

Secret whispers

Slight strength

Belief in the highest good

Harm no one

Embrace the pathways

Of the old ones

The Ancients.

Magick is real

And rituals-spellwork is

Similar to Prayer

Only intentions differ.

Divination

Is a journey and insight

Comes from within.

Moshi 7/9/19

Shiba Inu

Fox like ears

Curly q of a tail

Stubborn floof

Constantly shedding

Adorable personality

Completely petable

Just shy of 30 pounds

Prefers howling to barking

Sesame red

Quirky but easy to train

Once trained will only respond

To commands if he's in the mood.

Prey driven chases small creatures

Affectionate and loyal

He's the King of all beasts.

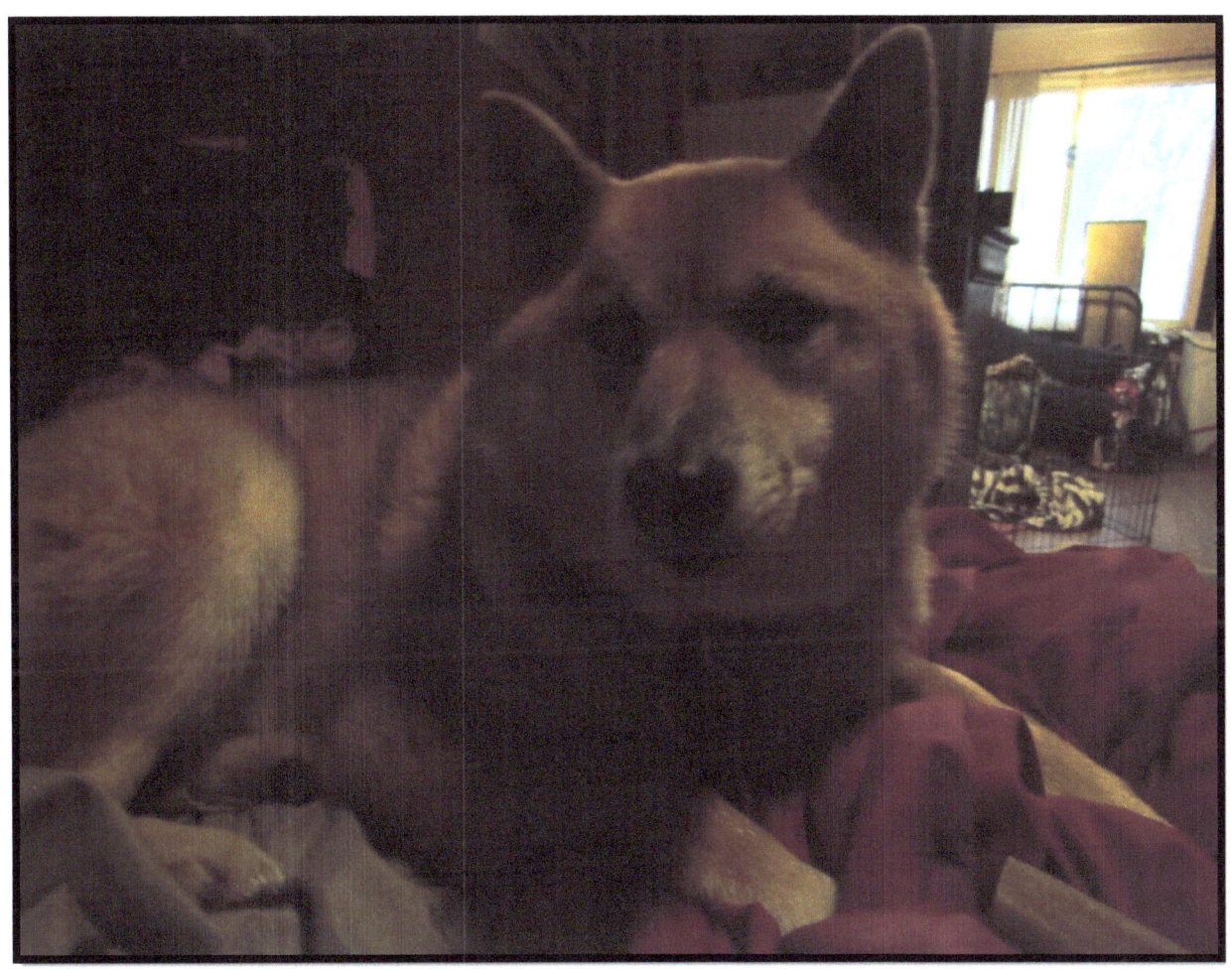

Summertime Part 2- 7/9/19

Summer is more than just weather.

It's the freedom of long sunny days

The coloring book blue skies

The plants you grow from seeds

Summer is when your skin sticks together

By sweat and dry heat.

And the breeze blows your hair

against your cheek.

Summer brings the 4th of July

Picnics get-togethers fireworks galore.

Lazy days

Barefoot walking through the grass and shore.

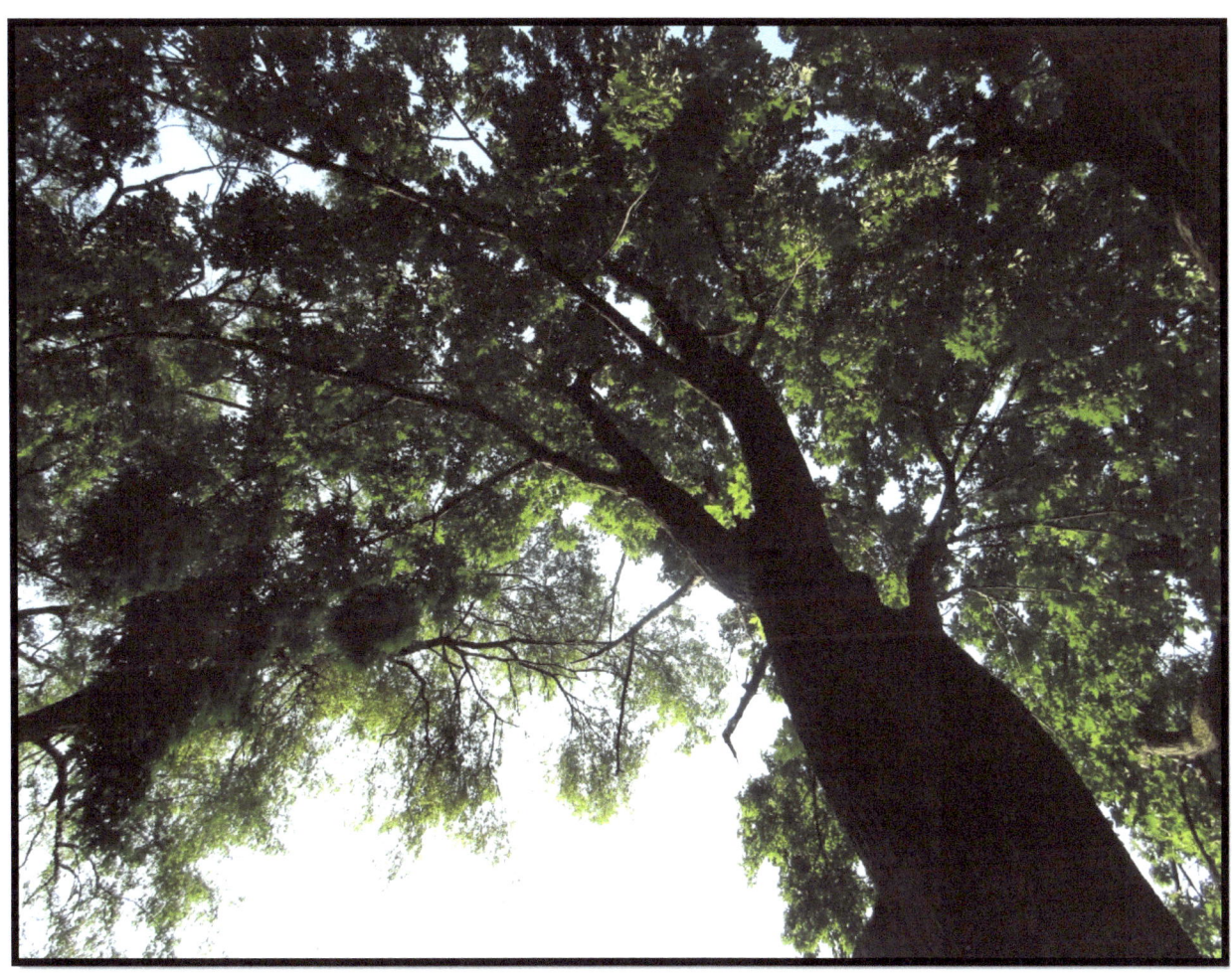

v. Grief and Loss

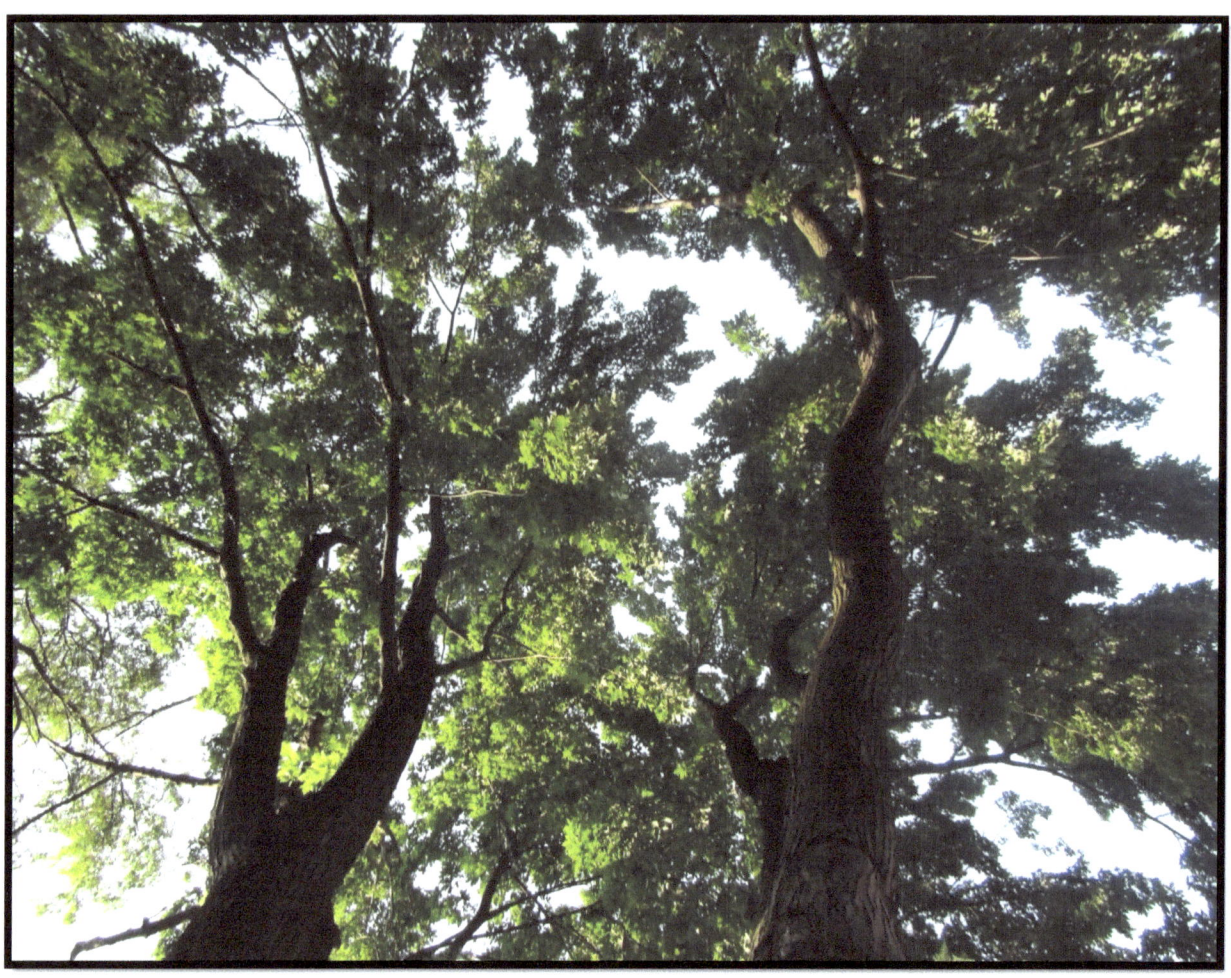

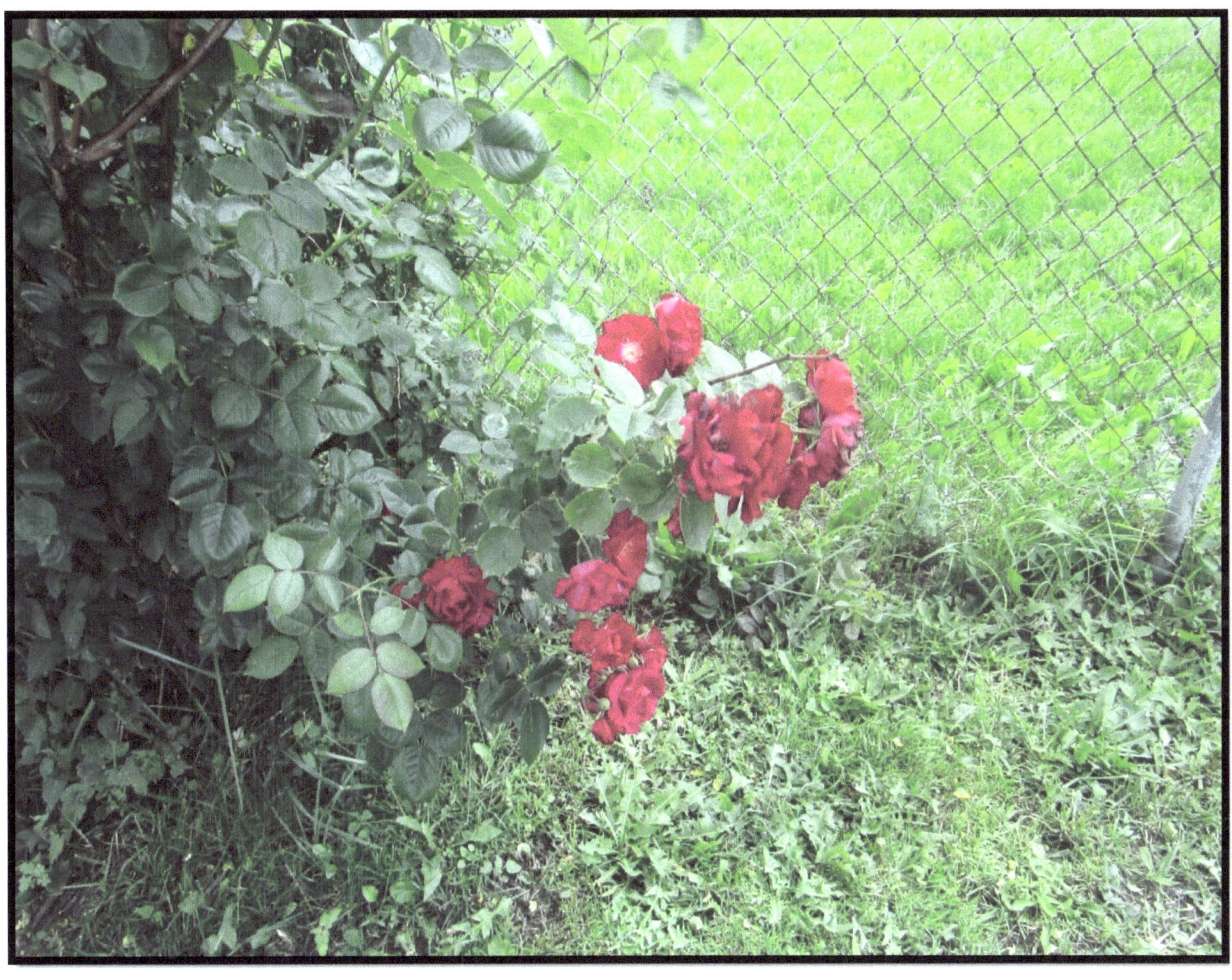

Roses don't grow

in concrete.

Love doesn't bloom

in the desert.

Warmth isn't found

in an iceberg

Roses don't grow

in concrete

But Rainbows only appear

after the thunderstorms.

I never asked you for roses

but after you stormed

I did expect

a rainbow.

Published on www.sexinthekitchensink.wordpress.com

Birthdays coming soon

Thunder heart

Beats of doom.

Cancers crashing

Not my own

Just somebody I love

My age is creeping

Twist turning to find

Hallowed ground.

Loved ones may

Die sometime soon.

Middle aged

45

Thickened this

Life soup spills

So soft and silently.

Birthday wishes

Bring

Disharmony.

Death whispers- 5/29/19

Death is on the doorstop.

Death is in my dreams,

and in my dreams Death whispers to me

there is nothing you can do

I will come for him.

I try to accept it as well it is what it is.

Death is coming and Cancer doesn't fight fairly.

Although I can't bear to witness or watch

Death is coming just the same.

Too many years we were estranged.

Not my choice but it was his.

Now nothing but a very fragile

Connection remains.

Death is on the doorstop.

Death is in my dreams.

In my dreams Death whispers to me,

There is nothing you can do

I will come for him.

Forgiveness- 5/29/19

Forgiveness is easy to say

but difficult to do.

When somebody you love

and trust completely cuts you,

out of their life for years yet

acts as though nothing has changed

except for everything that has and did in fact change.

How do you forgive this gasping wide hole

That they left in your heart?

I will always be

The pretty black sheep

The face of stigma

The mentally-ill daughter.

And he will always be the absent Father.

But he's terminally ill now and I realize

I must forgive

Because Cancer is killing him very painfully

And very rapidly

It's like a semi-automatic.

He's riddled with

Cancer bullets.

And I don't know how to forgive

But the clocks ticking

Away like a time-bomb

And I'm unsure of how much time

He has left

Before

It simply all blows to Hell

And my Daddy's gone.

Stampede- 6/8/19

Sunsets

Fade within hours.

Moments can feel,

like time standing still

especially when you are young.

As you grow older

Those moments pass by so much quicker.

The hoof beats

Of a racing clock can run you down,

if you're not careful.

A runaway horse

Can gallop away

A lifetime of moments,

in just a few seconds.

Before you realize it,

Years become

Dust in your hands and gray in your hair.

Try to enjoy what time you have

And enjoy it for the

Gift it is.

VI. Love

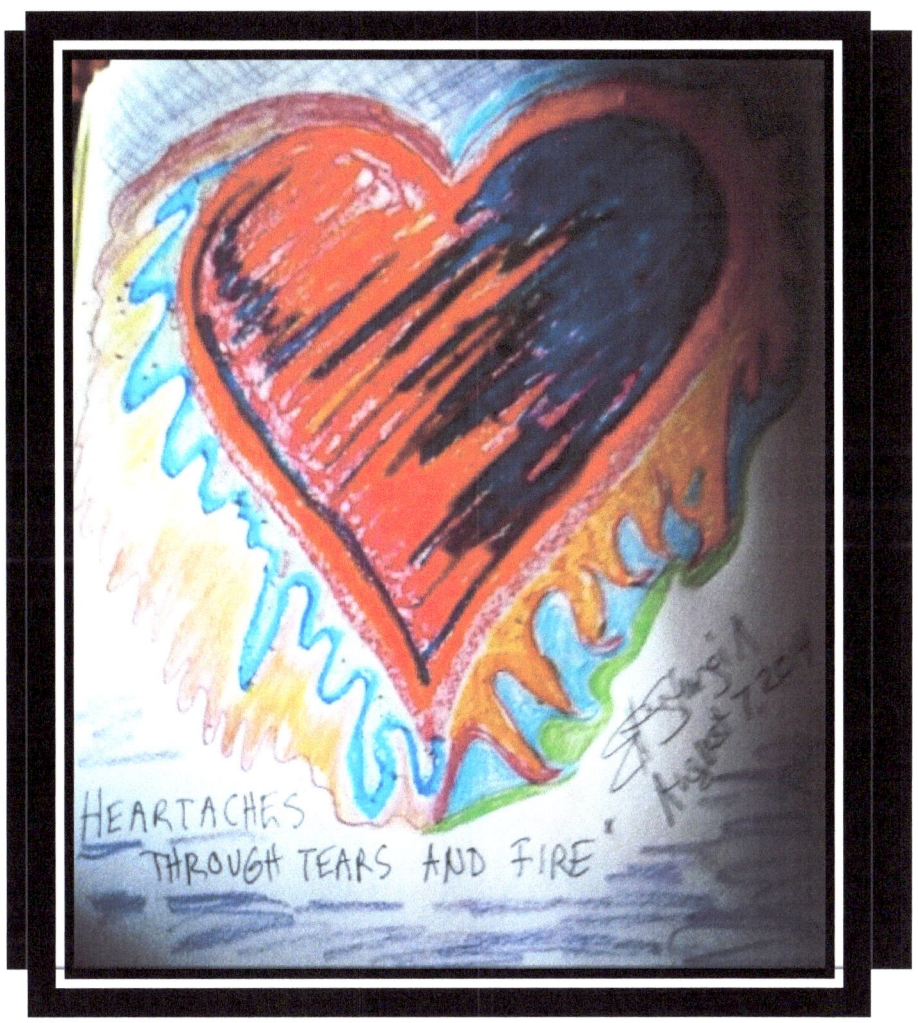

Soul Mate- 10/21/18

He is my rock solid.

He is my better half.

He is the Algebra in my equation

That equals perfect math.

He is my best friend.

He is my morning song.

His heart is my home.

Somewhere we both belong.

He is my husband.

His star is bright

and sincere.

He has the bluest eyes,

They reflect a sea.

A soul so deep

The blue of a thousand skies.

I get lost in a stare.

And marriage is

A promise we keep

A love that binds.

Bricks- 6/8/19

A feeling so fleeting,

I pluck it out of the air.

A doubt or a worry,

I really don't care.

The scale slips,

the feelings flip.

Amidst emotions,

lost potions

of romance,

burn anew.

The candle or flame,

Leaving burns-my heart,

only has you.

Words say so very less.

Labels don't stick-

heart this I feel

like a ton of bricks.

Earthquake- 10/21/18

Published on www.sexinthekitchensink.wordpress.com

My body trembles,

when you say my name

with a simple touch,

I resolve to dust.

As we make love,

the Earth shifts on it's axis,

as I rotate slightly

beneath the warmth

of your Sun.

Everything

Everything

It's Everything shaking.

You feel hard

You feel large

You feel like,

      My Earthquake baby.

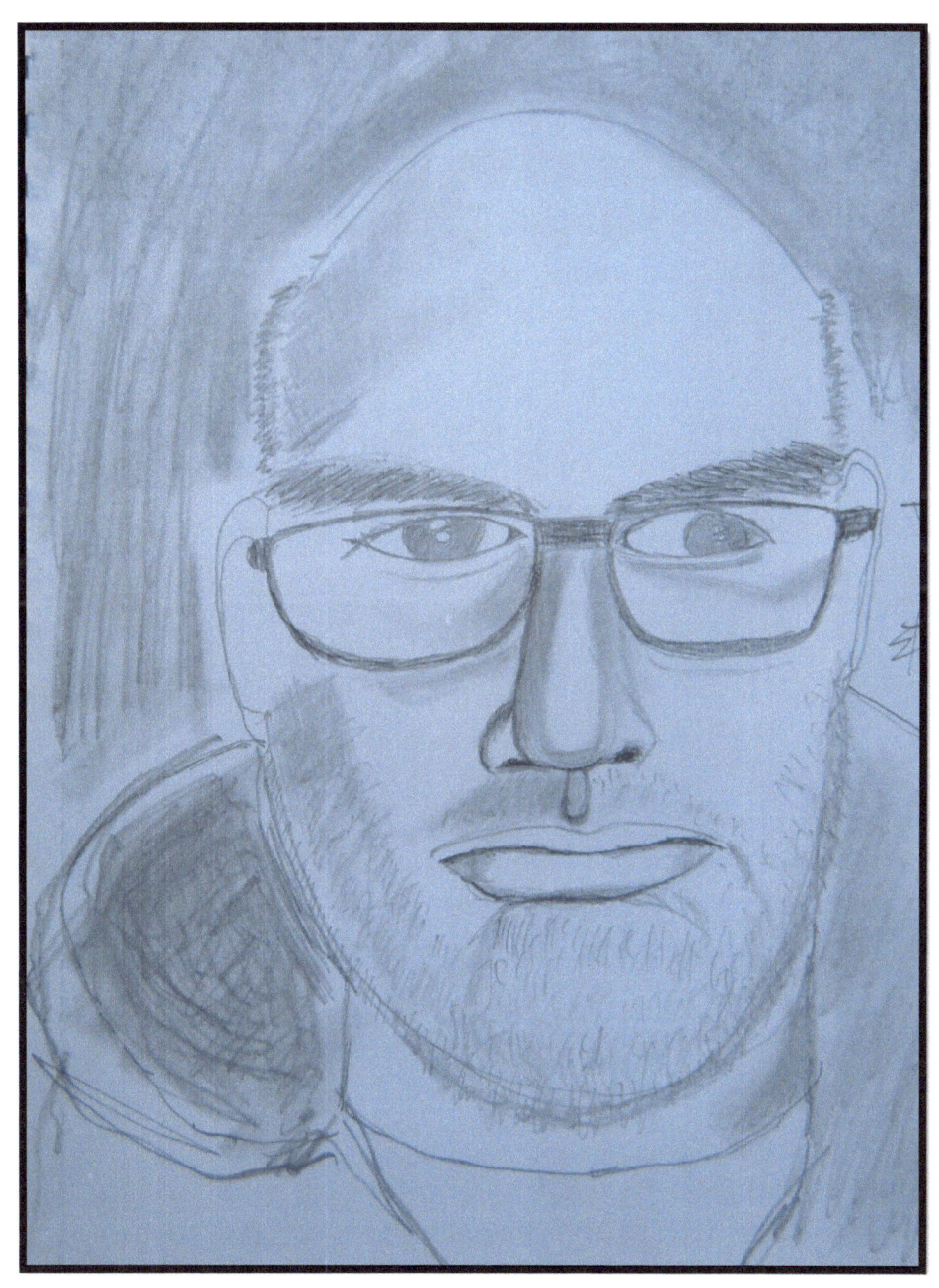

vii. Acknowledgements

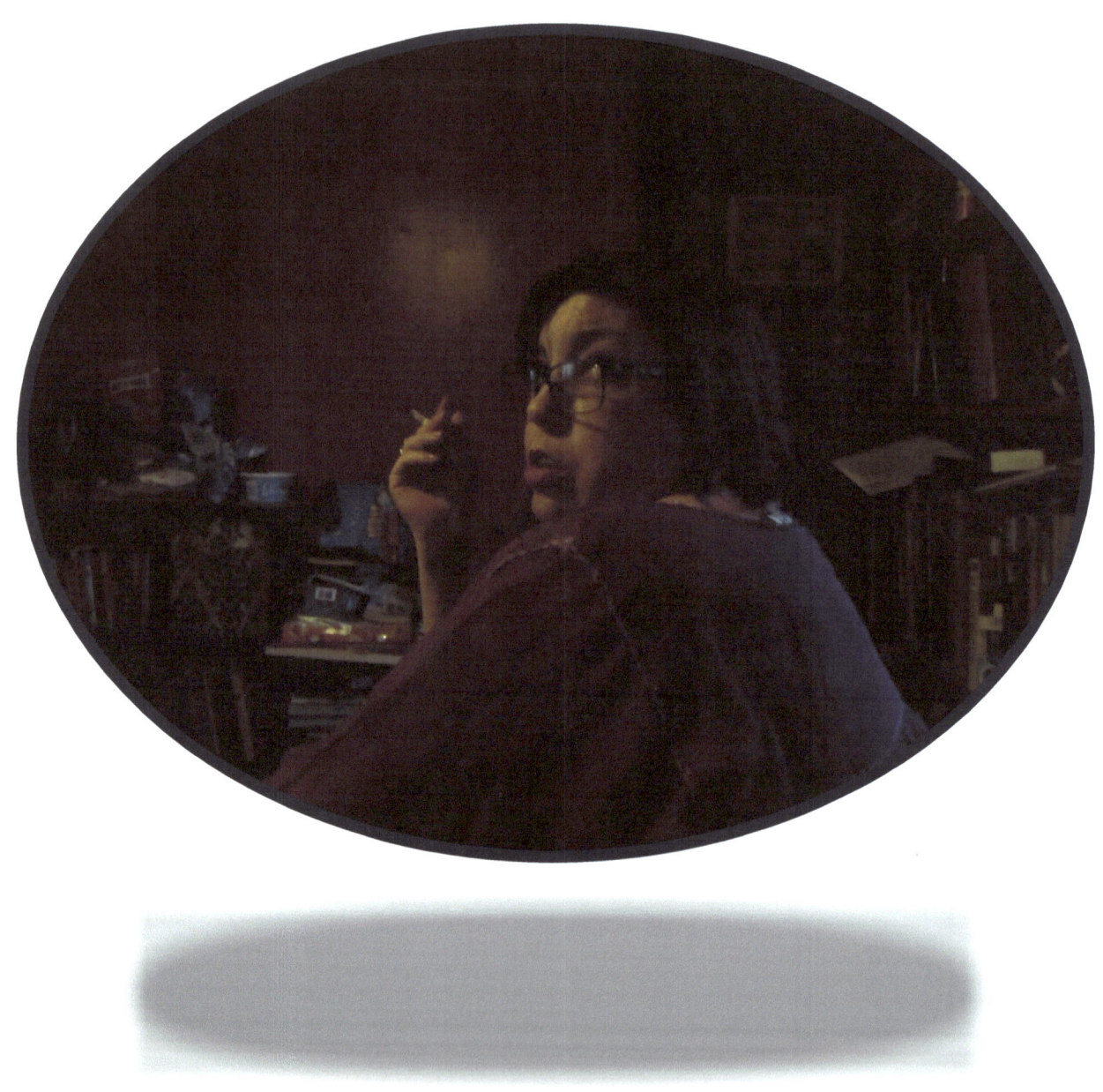

Gratitude and Many thanks to the following:

My followers of my poetry blog at www.sexinthekitchensink.com. My followers on my Facebook page

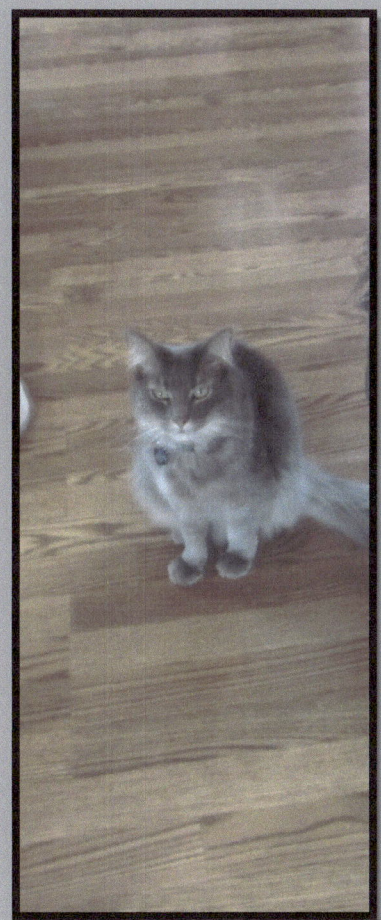

Sex in the Kitchen Sink Modern Poetry and Artwork. My readers on Amazon Kindle. My friends, my husband and my family. My two doggies and two kitties that are my world.

When I first started my blog in 2012 I never thought anyone would read it. When I wrote my first artist and poetry chapbook Sex in the kitchen Sink poetry and artwork I didn't think anyone would read that either. I'm very glad I was wrong. It's been a long time since I've self published anything at all.

This is merely a small offering. I dedicate this book to all the artists, poets, writers and the dreamers. I also dedicate this book to anyone who struggles with physical or mental illness. You inspire me to speak out, to be brave and deal with things head on. Thank you for reading this book. Thank you for your time.

Sincerely,

Emily H, Sturgill

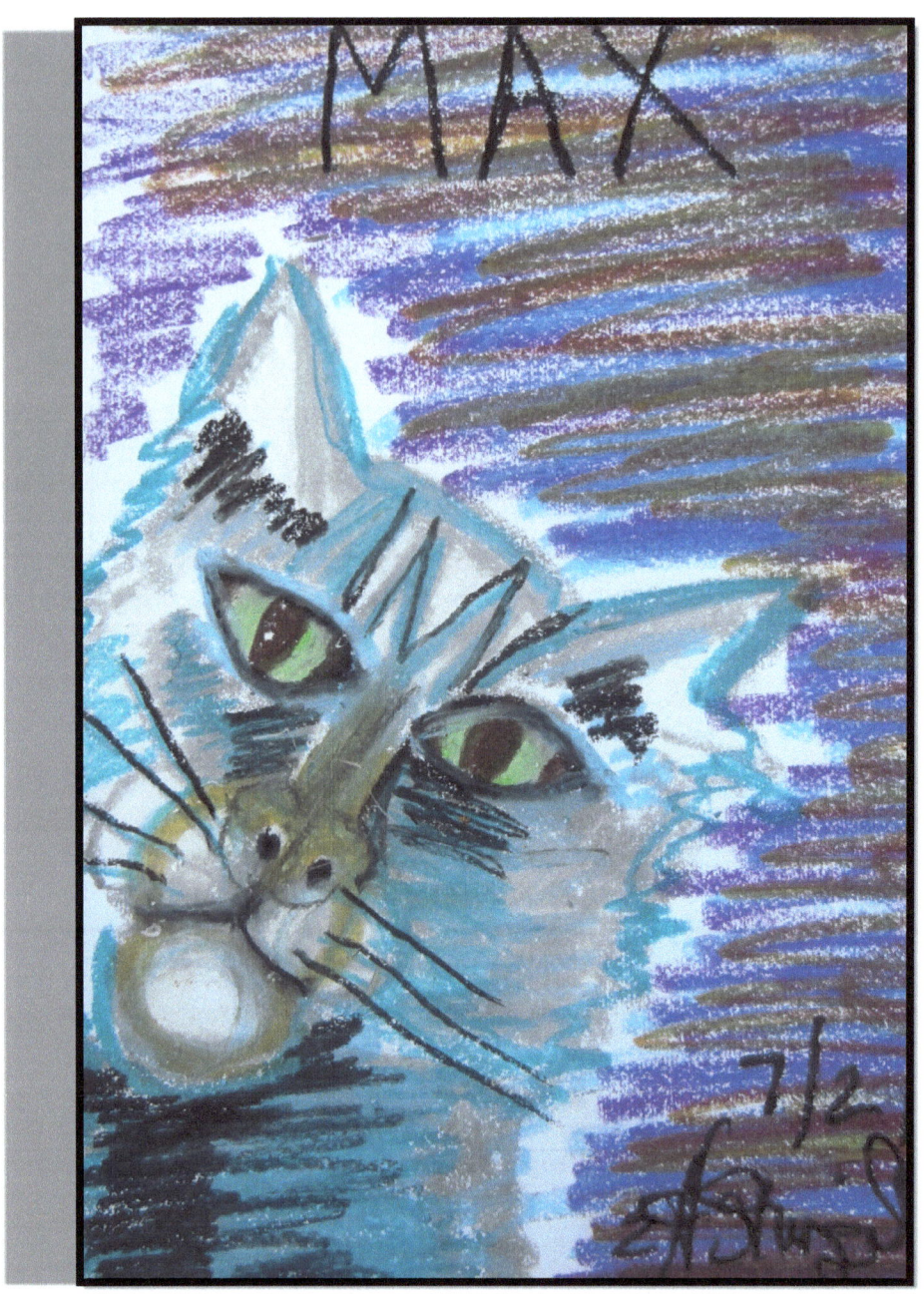

List of artworks and photographs: All artworks and photographs by Emily H.Sturgill unless otherwise noted.

"Music warming up." Mixed media, 2/24/19, page 3.

"Black coffee and music." Oil pastels, 1/9/19, page 6.

"Photograph of Bleeding heart bush." Photography, May 2019, page 7.

" Portrait of a Rose." Photography, May 2019, page12..

"Roses Abstraction." Oil paint and paper tissue on canvas, 2012, page 21.

"Two Paintings: Manic-Depression." Oil on canvas, 2006, page 22.

"Goldfish pond." Photograph, June 2019, page 30.

"Waiting for spring." Oil pastels, 1/5/19, page 32.

"Irises" Colored pencil, 2012, page 35.

" Portrait of Isis." Photography, June 2019., page 37.

"Portrait of Isis." Oil pastels, 2/2/19, page 39.

"Still life with crystals and a candle." Photography 7/11/19, page 41.

" Portrait of Moshi." Photography, May 2019, page 44.

"Tree No.1" Photography, 7/9/19, page 46.

"Rose bush." Photography, May 2019, page 48.

"Heartaches through tears and fire."Oil pastel drawing, 2014, page 56.

"Portrait of my husband." Pencil drawing, 4/15/19, page 60.

"Portrait of Emily H. Sturgill." Photography by Dean Sturgill, May 2019, page 61.

"Portraits of Mystique and Max," Photography of my kitties, 7/9/19, page 61 and page 65..

"Portrait of Max." Oil pastels, 7/2/19, page 63..

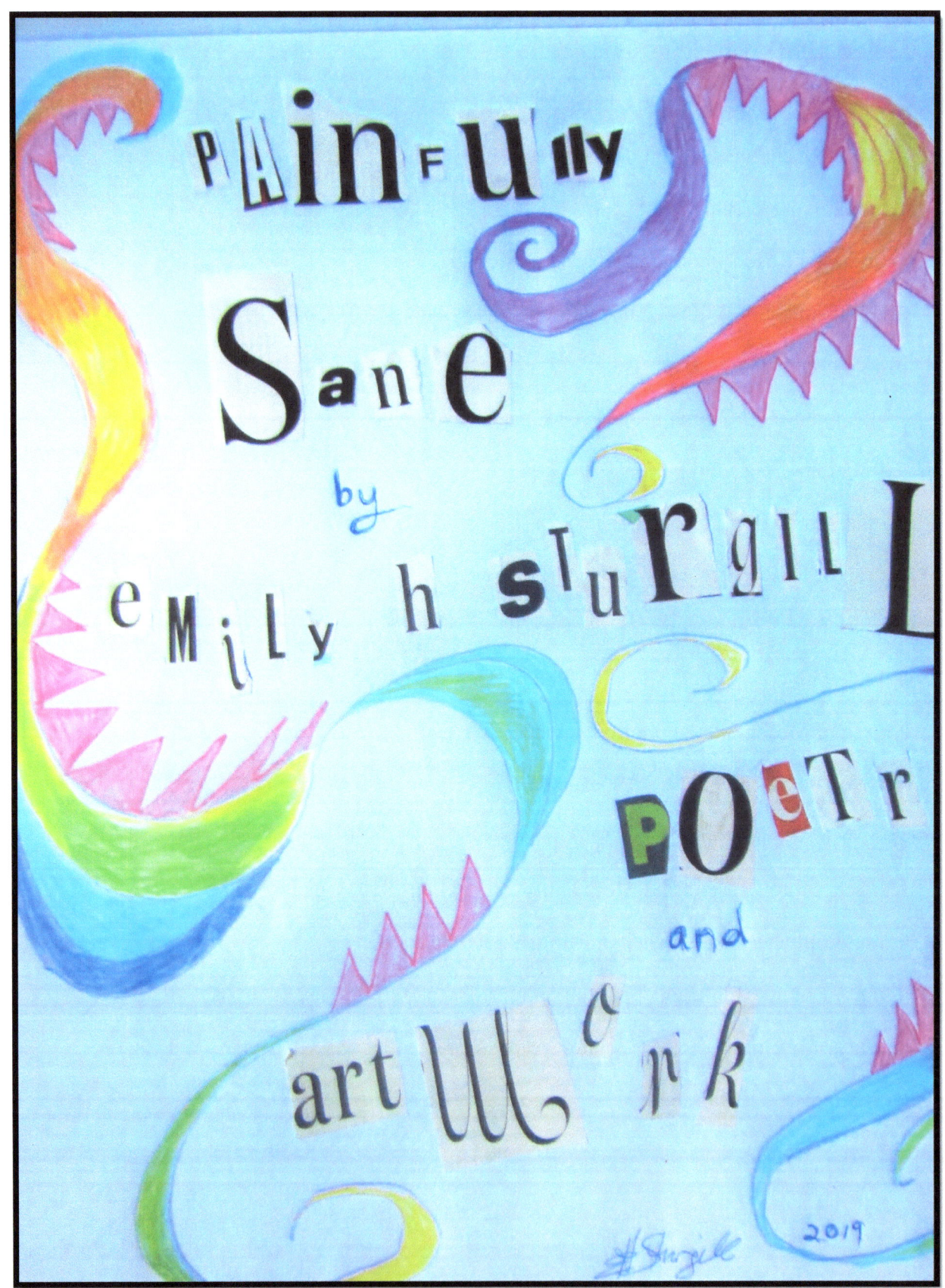

Cover Art design by Emily H. Sturgill, Mixed Media magazine collage and colored pencils, 7/10/19.

Painfully Sane: Poetry and Artwork by Emily H.Sturgill

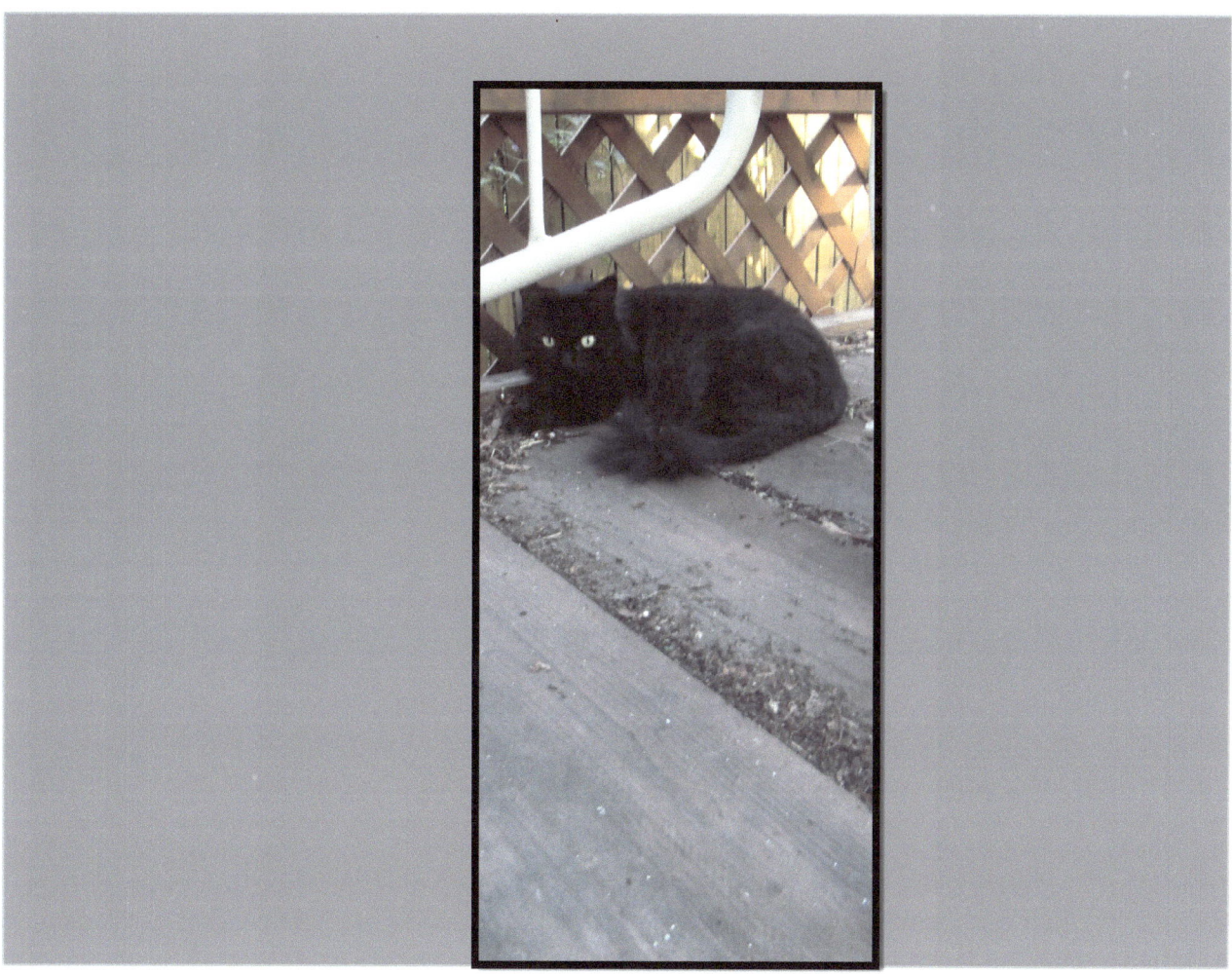

www.ingramcontent.com/pod-product-compliance
Lightning Source LLC
Chambersburg PA
CBHW051045180526
45172CB00002B/529